WakeUP to Your W.O.W.!® Unleash Your Inner Power and Live Your Best Life

WakeUP to Your W.O.W.!®

ISBN: 979-8-9929340-0-7

Cover and Interior Design: Sheryll Mizell

Printed in the United States.

This Journal Belongs To

____

____

____

____

Introduction

I'm delighted to welcome you to the WakeUP to Your W.O.W!® Empowerment Journal! This journal is crafted to guide high-performing women like you through a transformative 30-day exploration, focusing on five essential pillars of personal growth: Positivity, Self-Love, Personal Expression, Self-Care, and Financial Empowerment. As you embark on this journey, you're not just investing in a tool for self-reflection; you're embracing an opportunity to elevate every facet of your life and ignite your inner power so you can WakeUP to Your Brilliance, Own Your Unique Power and Win Wildly with Purpose.

Why You Should Wake Up to Your W.O.W.!®

At WakeUP to Your W.O.W.!®, we believe that every person has an extraordinary, untapped potential—your WOW. It's that spark inside of you, the greatness that is just waiting to be unleashed. But let's be real: life can sometimes dim that light. Whether it's the challenges of the pandemic, everyday stress, or just the chaos of modern living, it's easy to lose sight of your true self and purpose.

We've all been there.

That's exactly why I created WakeUP to Your W.O.W.!®—because I understand the transformative power of reigniting that spark and rediscovering your joy, your self-worth, and your purpose.

When you wake up to your WOW, you're embracing the full spectrum of who you are—the good, the challenging, and the extraordinary. You'll learn how to honor your health, build a mindset of abundance, and love yourself fiercely. This journey is not about getting by; it's about thriving—confidently stepping into your power and living a life that feels as amazing on the inside as it looks on the outside.

Have you ever wondered what it would feel like to truly live at your highest potential? To not just survive, but to thrive? Imagine waking up every day feeling energized, aligned with your purpose, and ready to conquer anything life throws at you. Sounds amazing, right? That's exactly what you're capable of when you Wake Up to Your WOW. But here's the thing—living at your full potential doesn't just happen by accident. It takes intentionality. It takes awareness. It takes action.

What would your life look like if you stopped holding back? Think about it: how much more confident, bold, and unstoppable would you feel if you stopped dimming your light to make others comfortable? You are meant to shine. And when you do, you're not just lighting up your own path—you're inspiring others to do the same. Imagine the ripple effect that could have.

We live in a world that often pushes us to do more, be more, and achieve more. But the question is: are you doing all of that from a place of true fulfillment? Or are you chasing after things just to keep up with the chaos of life? I**t's time to take a step back, breathe, and ask yourself: What would it look like if you finally put yourself first?** You are your greatest asset—don't forget that!

Let's talk about mindset for a second. You've heard the saying, "What you think, you become." Well, it's true. Your mindset is everything! If you're always thinking you're not enough, that you can't achieve your dreams, or that something is always holding you back —guess what? That's exactly what you'll manifest. But when you shift to a mindset of abundance, possibilities open up. The universe responds to the energy you put out. **So, how about it—ready to raise your vibe and invite the best into your life?**

You don't have to have it all figured out today. This journey is about progress, not perfection. **Rome wasn't built in a day, and neither is your best self.** So, let's start with one step at a time. What's one small thing you can do today to align your actions with the life you truly want to create? Maybe it's a new self-care ritual, a positive affirmation, or simply taking a moment to appreciate your own brilliance. Small steps lead to massive change!

Life doesn't have to be a grind, you know. We've been conditioned to believe that hard work means sacrifice, that success has to come with a cost. But what if I told you that success can actually be fun? That you can achieve your goals without losing yourself in the process? It's time to shake off the old narrative and start writing your own story—a story where you get to have it all: joy, fulfillment, success, and a whole lot of WOW.

t

What This Journal is All About

In this journal, you'll embark on a journey to reclaim your inner strength, rediscover your passion, and align your daily actions with your highest potential. Each day's prompt will help you delve into one of the five key themes:

- **Positivity:** Cultivating an optimistic outlook and finding silver linings in challenging situations. It's about developing a mindset that embraces growth and resilience.
- **Self-Love:** Recognizing your worth and treating yourself with kindness and respect. This involves celebrating your achievements and nurturing your well-being.
- **Personal Expression:** Owning your voice and confidently sharing your unique perspectives. It's about aligning your actions with your true self.
- **Self-Care:** Implementing practices that rejuvenate and restore your physical, emotional, and mental health. It's essential for maintaining balance and energy.
- **Financial Empowerment:** Taking control of your financial situation and making informed decisions to achieve security and freedom. This involves planning, setting goals, and understanding your financial landscape.

Throughout this journey, you'll find that the prompts are not just about introspection but also about actionable steps. They are designed to help you weave these themes into your daily life, ensuring that your growth is not confined to the pages of this journal but reflected in your everyday actions and decisions. By the end of this 30-day journey, you'll have a clearer vision of your personal and professional goals, a deeper sense of self-awareness, and a renewed commitment to living a balanced and empowered life.

Why Use This Journal?

Engaging with this journal can lead to greater self-awareness, enhanced well-being, and a clearer path to achieving your goals. Whether you're new to journaling or a seasoned writer, the daily quotes and prompts are designed to inspire and support your journey. By dedicating time each day to reflection and action, you can foster a deeper connection with yourself and create meaningful change. The power of this journal lies in its ability to transform your daily routines into intentional practices that elevate your life and align it with your core values.

Notes on How to Use This Journal

To make the most of your Empowerment Journey, follow these simple steps:

- **Daily Reflection:** Start each day by reading the quote and message provided. Allow the theme to resonate with you before engaging with the daily prompt. This initial reflection helps set a positive tone and primes your mind for meaningful exploration.
- **Engage with the Prompt:** Use the prompt to explore your thoughts, feelings, and actions related to that day's theme. Write freely and honestly to uncover insights and solutions. Remember, there are no right or wrong answers—this is your personal space to discover and express.
- **Stay Consistent:** Dedicate a few minutes each day to this journaling practice. Consistency will help you build habits and achieve lasting change. Even on busy days, a brief reflection can be powerful and maintain the momentum of your journey.
- **Review and Reflect:** At the end of the 30 days, revisit your entries and reflect on your growth. Consider how you can continue to apply the insights you've gained to your daily life. This review process will help consolidate your progress and plan future steps.
- **Celebrate Your Journey:** Acknowledge and celebrate your progress. Each step you take toward empowerment is a victory, and recognizing your achievements will fuel your continued growth. Celebrating your milestones, big or small, reinforces your commitment and motivates you to keep moving forward.

A Heartfelt Reminder

As you navigate through this journal, remember to be gentle with yourself. This space is designed for your reflection and growth, but it's crucial to approach it with self-compassion. If you encounter prompts that stir strong emotions or present challenges, give yourself permission to pause and seek support if necessary. Your well-being is top priority, and nurturing your emotional needs is essential as you embark on this journey of self-discovery and empowerment.

Let Me Introduce Myself…

My name is Sheryll Mizell, and I'm passionate about empowering high-achieving women, leaders and entrepreneurs to find balance, embrace self-care, and harness their full potential. I created this journal to blend practical wisdom with inspirational insights, providing you with a powerful tool for personal growth. My goal is for this journal to be a valuable companion on your path to empowerment, offering guidance and support as you navigate the complexities of your journey. I believe that through this journal, you will uncover new strengths, set meaningful goals, and achieve a sense of fulfillment that resonates deeply within you.

Let's Connect!

I would love to hear about your journey with this journal. Feel free to connect with me at **mizellcan@gmail.com** and share your experiences. Your feedback not only helps you reflect but also inspires others who are on a similar path. Engaging with our community can provide additional support and encouragement as you progress through your empowerment journey.

Wishing you an empowering and transformative journey!

Warmly,

Sheryll Mizell,
Author of the WakeUP to Your W.O.W!® Empowerment Journal

Introduction: Welcome to the start of your journey toward a more balanced and fulfilling life! Today, let's take a moment to reflect on how you're feeling about your work-life balance. Understanding where you are now is the first step in making positive changes.

Self-reflection is not always easy, but it is a powerful act of self-awareness. It invites you to slow down and listen to what your body, mind, and spirit are trying to communicate. As a high-performing woman, you're used to pushing forward, juggling responsibilities, and showing up for everyone else. Today, the invitation is to turn inward and show up for you.

Think of this moment as a personal check-in. What emotions have been lingering beneath the surface? What patterns have you noticed—feeling energized at work but depleted at home, or constantly multitasking without truly feeling present? Naming these experiences with compassion allows you to gain clarity, and that clarity is where real change begins.

As you move through this journal, let this first step anchor you. You don't have to have it all figured out—this is about progress, not perfection. By acknowledging how you truly feel right now, you're laying the groundwork for the aligned, joyful life you deserve. Take a deep breath and give yourself full permission to be honest, gentle, and brave.

Self-Reflection

Prompt: Describe how you currently feel about your work-life balance. What are the biggest sources of stress or burnout in your life?

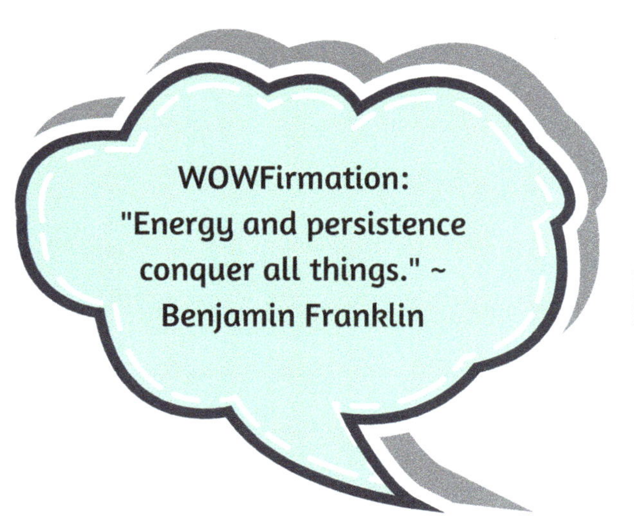

Day 2

Energy Inventory

Introduction: Feeling drained? You're not alone. Today, let's pinpoint what's zapping your energy and think about how to create a bit more space for the things that rejuvenate you.

Your energy is your most valuable currency. When it's depleted, everything feels harder—your focus, your patience, even your joy. By identifying what drains you, you gain power. You get to choose where your energy goes, and just as importantly, what no longer deserves it.

As a high-performing woman, you likely carry responsibilities that stretch you in every direction. But not everything that demands your attention is worthy of it. Some things—and people—are energy leaks. This isn't about judgment; it's about awareness. Knowing what takes from you allows you to intentionally fill back up.

Where does your energy naturally expand—and where does it shrink? Are there tasks, relationships, or routines that leave you feeling depleted, even resentful? Consider how you can begin to draw firmer boundaries, delegate more often, or let go of what no longer aligns with your values and well-being. You don't need to do it all to be enough.

Let today be your opportunity to reclaim your energy. Protect it like you would your time or money. Because when your energy is protected and directed with intention, you not only survive—you thrive. And that thriving version of you is who the world truly needs.

Energy Inventory

Prompt: List three activities or people that drain your energy.
How can you minimize their impact on your day?

Day 3

Self-Care Priorities

Introduction: Self-care isn't a luxury; it's a necessity. Today, we're going to identify your top self-care needs. Let's get real about what makes you feel refreshed and how to weave those practices into your routine.

Think of self-care as your non-negotiable foundation, not a reward for burnout. It's not just about bubble baths or spa days—it's also setting boundaries, saying no, resting without guilt, and nourishing your body, mind, and soul in ways that matter to you.

When you prioritize yourself, you model to others that you are worthy of care, attention, and tenderness. And you are. You don't have to earn your rest or prove your productivity to deserve peace. The real power move is choosing yourself first so you can serve from a full cup.

You are not selfish for needing space. You are strategic. When you invest in your wellness, you reclaim time, energy, and clarity. What routines or habits have you neglected that actually sustain your spirit? This is your moment to redefine what care means for you, not just what the world tells you it should be.

Ask yourself: What would it look like to treat your well-being like a business priority? What shifts would you make this week if you truly believed your needs were valid? Let today be your reminder: You are allowed to choose you.

Self-Care Priorities

Prompt: Write down your top three self-care needs.
How can you start integrating them into your daily routine?

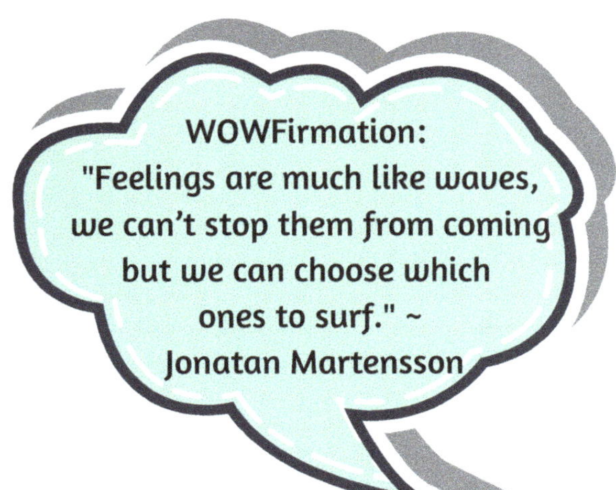

Day 4

Emotion Check-In

Introduction: Emotions can be overwhelming, especially when juggling a high-powered job and family life. Today, let's look back at a recent emotional challenge and explore how you managed it and what you might try next time.

Our emotions offer messages and insight. They reveal what we value, what needs attention, and where we might still be healing. Checking in with how you really feel —without judgment—gives you the space to move forward in alignment with your truth.

You don't have to suppress or control every feeling. Sometimes, it's enough to name the emotion, sit with it, and ask, "What do I need right now?" Emotional intelligence starts with awareness, and you're building that muscle right now.

There is power in processing, not perfection. Let today remind you that you can hold space for your own experience and also grow from it. You are not your emotions— you are the wise observer learning how to ride the waves with grace.

Your emotions aren't weaknesses—they're wisdom in motion. When you pause to feel with intention, you respond with clarity, not chaos. Today, give yourself the grace to listen deeply, honor what's real, and trust that even the heaviest waves are guiding you to steadier ground.

Emotion Check-In

Prompt: Reflect on a recent emotional challenge.
How did you handle it, and what would you do differently next time?

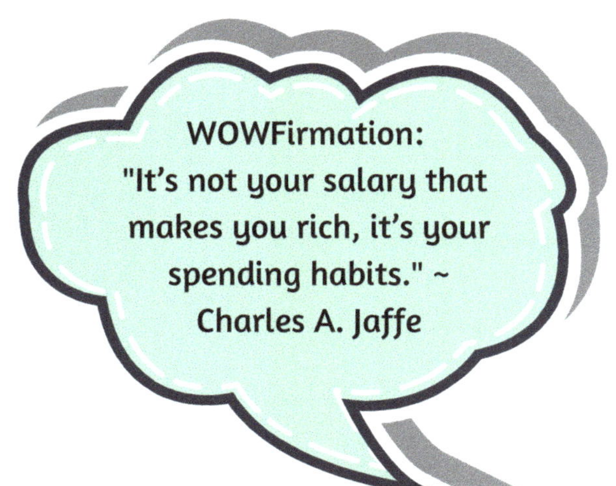

Day 5

Financial Clarity

Introduction: Money matters can sometimes feel like a huge stressor. Today, we're going to take a closer look at your financial situation and identify one area that might need more attention.

Financial clarity is more than just numbers—it's a form of self-trust. When you understand where your money is going, you gain control over your future instead of reacting in the moment. It's not about guilt or scarcity, but about choosing to be empowered. Clarity begins with awareness. Set aside a quiet moment to check in with your current financial habits—without judgment. Are there subscriptions you've forgotten about? Are your purchases reflecting your priorities and values? Awareness leads to intention, and intention fuels change.

As women, we're often taught to avoid money talk, but true empowerment includes financial literacy. Whether it's tracking spending, adjusting a budget, or planning for a goal, today's small step is a vote for your long-term peace and prosperity.

Remember, you don't have to overhaul everything overnight. Even one intentional shift—like reviewing your bank statement, setting a mini savings goal, or creating a mindful money mantra—can spark a ripple effect that affirms your worthiness for abundance, security, and freedom. Be gentle with yourself as you explore this. Financial wellness is a journey, not a destination. You don't have to be perfect—you just need to be present and willing to take the next right step.

Financial Clarity

Prompt: Evaluate your current financial situation.
What is one area where you feel stressed or uncertain?

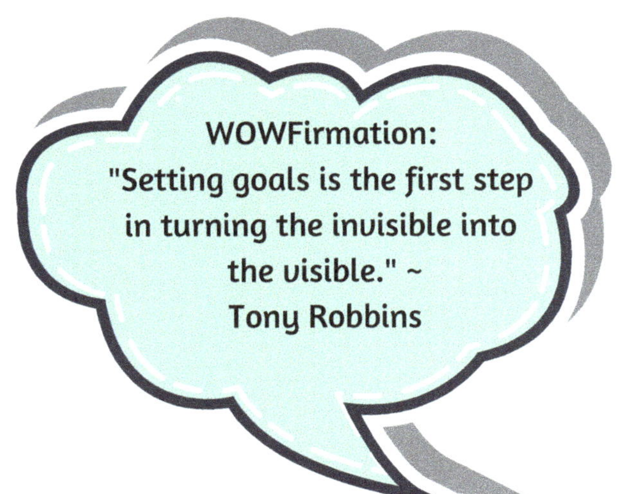

Goal Setting

Introduction: Setting goals can give you a sense of direction and purpose. Today, let's focus on defining one personal and one professional goal for the coming month. Think about the steps you need to take to achieve them.

Goals help you move with intention instead of just motion. They transform wishful thinking into action. When you clarify your desires, you start creating a life aligned with your values—not just your obligations.

It's okay to dream big and start small. In fact, that's often where the magic lives. What would success look like if it felt good to pursue? What do you want more of in your life, and what actions support that?

This is your reminder that you are both the architect and the masterpiece. Define what matters to you—and let your goals reflect that bold, beautiful vision.

Every meaningful goal starts with self-trust—the belief that your desires matter and your journey is enough. You don't need perfection to make progress—just the courage to begin. Let your goals be a reflection of who you're becoming, rooted in purpose and flexible with life's flow. Start small, stay aligned, and trust that each step forward is shaping something powerful.

Goal Setting

Prompt: Set one personal and one professional goal for the next month. What specific steps can you take to achieve these goals?

Day 7

Time Management

Introduction: Feeling like there's never enough time? Let's review your weekly schedule today. We'll find opportunities to create a better balance between work and personal time.

Time is your most precious asset. And how you spend it reveals what you value—intentionally or not. The goal isn't to do more, but to align your time with what matters most.

When you take back ownership of your calendar, you take back ownership of your life. What can be delegated, postponed, or released altogether? What would it feel like to schedule joy, not just tasks?

Remember, busy doesn't always mean productive. Let today be the day you choose to honor your time as sacred—and begin living accordingly.

Just like you budget your money, you can budget your minutes. Are you investing in what energizes and fulfills you—or just reacting to demands? Even 15 intentional minutes can shift the tone of your day. Time freedom isn't about doing less—it's about doing more of what truly matters.

You are not just managing a schedule—you're designing a life. One aligned hour can be more impactful than a full day spent out of sync. Treat your time like the limited, valuable resource it is, and use it to build a rhythm that supports your well-being, goals, and joy.

Time Management

Prompt: Review your weekly schedule. Identify any time blocks that can be adjusted to create more balance between work and personal life.

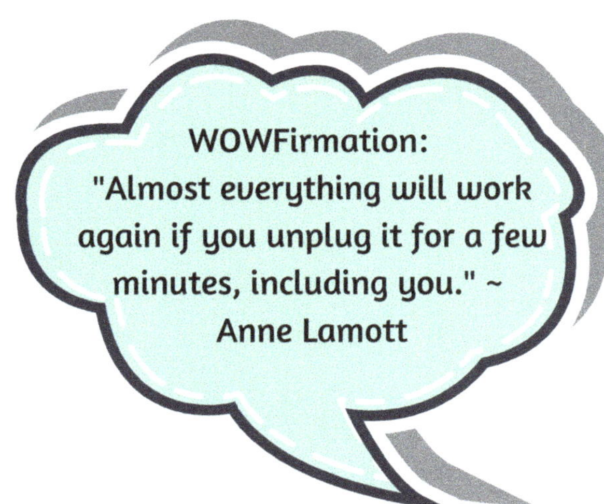

Recharge Routine

Introduction: Everyone needs time to recharge. Today, let's discover an activity that restores your energy and plan how to fit it into your busy week.

Your recharge routine doesn't need to be extravagant—it just needs to be intentional. Whether it's a walk outside, a dance break, or ten minutes of quiet time, giving yourself space to breathe is powerful.

You are not a machine. Your value isn't tied to your output. And rest is not laziness—it's preparation. Think of your recharge as fuel for your purpose, not a detour from it.
Today, give yourself permission to pause. Rest is not what you earn once everything's done—it's what allows you to keep going in alignment and peace.

Your body and mind are always speaking—burnout whispers long before it screams. When you build in space to consistently restore, you create a rhythm that honors your humanity and your ambition. Recharging regularly helps you show up clear-headed, more focused, and emotionally grounded.

This isn't indulgence—it's intelligence. High performers protect their energy like a CEO guards a company's assets. Prioritize your peace not as a luxury, but as a leadership strategy. When you thrive, everything around you benefits.

Recharge Routine

Prompt: Describe a simple activity that helps you recharge.
How can you incorporate this into your weekly routine?

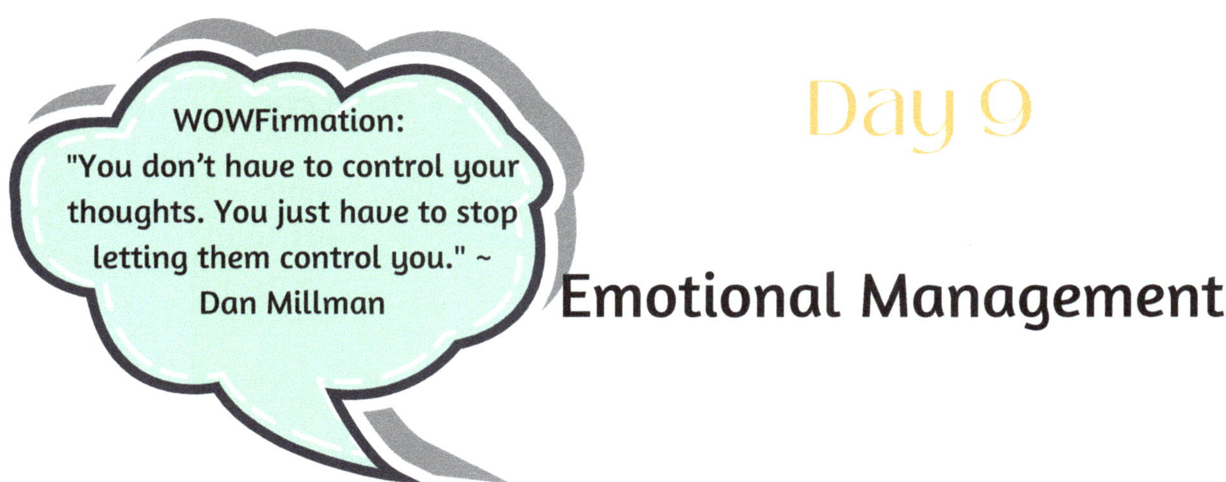

Day 9

Emotional Management

Introduction: Managing emotions effectively is crucial for maintaining balance. List some strategies that work for you and brainstorm ways to apply them more consistently.

We all have emotional triggers—what matters is how we respond. Emotional management is about cultivating tools, not perfection. Deep breaths, journaling, movement, and self-talk are all forms of self-support. There's no shame in feeling deeply. Emotions are messengers, and your job is to listen, not silence them. The more consistently you practice your strategies, the more confident and calm you'll feel in stressful moments.Today, recommit to your emotional toolkit. You already have wisdom within—this is just a reminder to use it with intention and love.

Emotional strength doesn't mean you're unshaken—it means you know how to return to center. When you normalize checking in with yourself, you create space between stimulus and response, where peace can live. That's where your power is. You are allowed to pause, process, and pivot. Leading with emotional intelligence is not just about managing feelings—it's about respecting them. Let your emotions guide, not govern, and choose compassion over control every time.

Think of your emotions like waves—they rise, peak, and pass. Suppressing them builds pressure, but naming what you feel without judgment helps disarm their intensity. You don't need a perfect process, just a present one. Each time you return to your emotional tools, you build resilience and self-trust which becomes your anchor.

Emotional Management

Prompt: List three strategies that help you manage your emotions effectively. How can you practice these strategies more consistently?

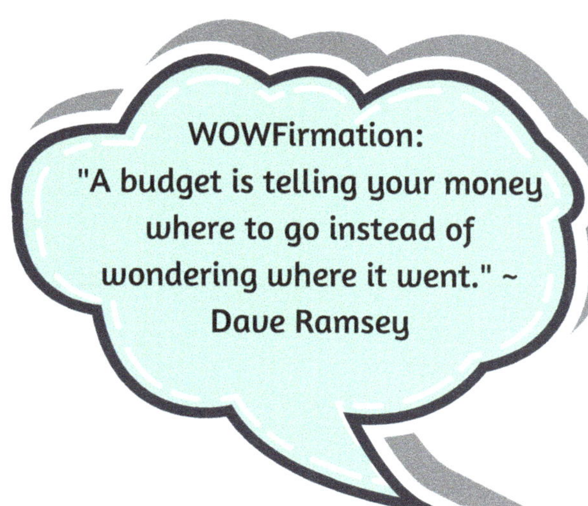

Day 10

Financial Planning

Introduction: A clear budget can bring peace of mind. Today, we'll outline a basic budget plan and look at ways to manage your money more effectively.

Budgeting isn't about restriction—it's about clarity and freedom. When you know your numbers, you can make confident choices, set aligned goals, and reduce financial stress. Start small and be real with yourself. What matters most to you? Are your spending habits reflecting your priorities, or are they reacting to external pressures? Adjustments can bring your budget into harmony with your dreams.

You are worthy of wealth, peace, and confidence with money. Let today be a powerful step toward owning your financial narrative. Your relationship with money is deeply personal. It's shaped by your experiences, beliefs, and even past wounds. But the good news? It can evolve. Give yourself grace as you create new habits rooted in self-awareness and self-worth.

Consistency beats perfection. Checking in with your finances weekly—even for just 10 minutes—can build trust in yourself. Small, steady actions create strong financial foundations and lasting change.

Remember, you're not just budgeting for bills—you're budgeting for your best life. Every dollar can be a vote for the life you desire. Use this moment to realign your money with your values, your vision, and your voice.

Financial Planning

Prompt: Outline a basic budget plan for the next month.
What are your main spending categories, and how can you optimize them?

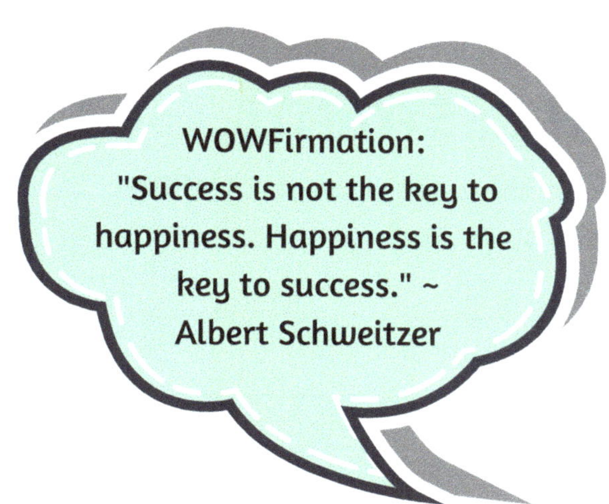

Day 11

Fulfillment Assessment

Introduction: Feeling fulfilled is a sign you're on the right track. Reflect on a recent accomplishment that made you feel proud and fulfilled, and let's explore what contributed to that sense of achievement.

Fulfillment runs deeper than success—it's that inner glow you feel when your actions align with your purpose. It's not always about big wins or applause; sometimes it's the quiet satisfaction of showing up for yourself, staying true to your values, or making a difference in someone's life. When you feel fulfilled, you feel whole—like your energy and effort actually matter.

Take a moment to revisit an experience that made you proud. What were you doing? Who were you being? Was it the result or the journey that gave you that sense of joy and purpose? Fulfillment is often found in the why behind the what—and when you recognize those moments, you unlock a map to your most authentic life.

Use today's reflection to identify the conditions that spark your fulfillment. These moments are clues. The more you understand what energizes and nourishes your spirit, the more empowered you become to build a life that feels as good as it looks.

Fulfillment Assessment

Prompt: Reflect on a recent accomplishment that made you feel fulfilled. What elements contributed to this feeling?

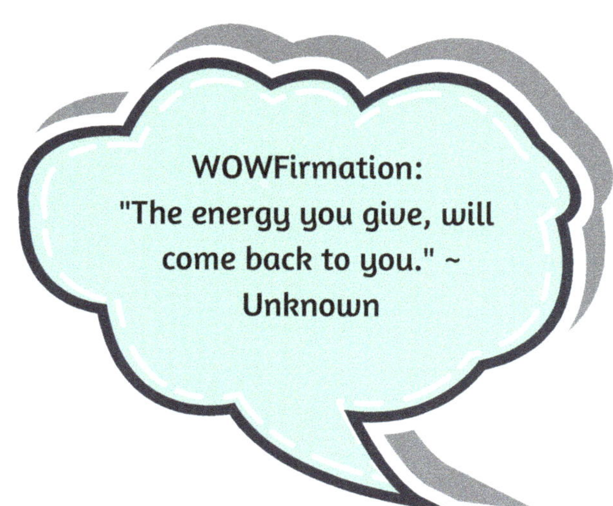

Personal Energy Boost

Introduction: We all need a boost sometimes. Identify a healthy habit that lifts your energy and plan to incorporate it into your daily routine at least three times this week.

Energy is more than just physical stamina—it's emotional, mental, and even spiritual. When you're energized, you show up more fully for your goals, relationships, and yourself. But when you're drained, even the smallest tasks can feel overwhelming. That's why it's essential to identify what fuels you.

Think of a habit or practice that leaves you feeling refreshed, centered, or more alive. Maybe it's a morning walk, drinking more water, journaling, dancing to your favorite playlist, or simply saying "no" to what no longer serves you. Notice what shifts your energy upward.

This week, challenge yourself to consciously integrate that boost at least three times. Watch how that intentional refueling not only enhances your mood—but also your mindset, motivation, and momentum. Your energy is your power source, and protecting it is an act of self-respect. Start noticing what drains you and what fills your cup. Who are you around? What are you consuming? How are you speaking to yourself? These small cues matter.

Small shifts, made with intention, can transform your day. You deserve to feel good, balanced, and empowered. You're not here just to get by—you're here to thrive, fueled by energy that sustains you.

Personal Energy Boost

Prompt: Identify a healthy habit that boosts your energy.
Plan to implement this habit at least three times this week.

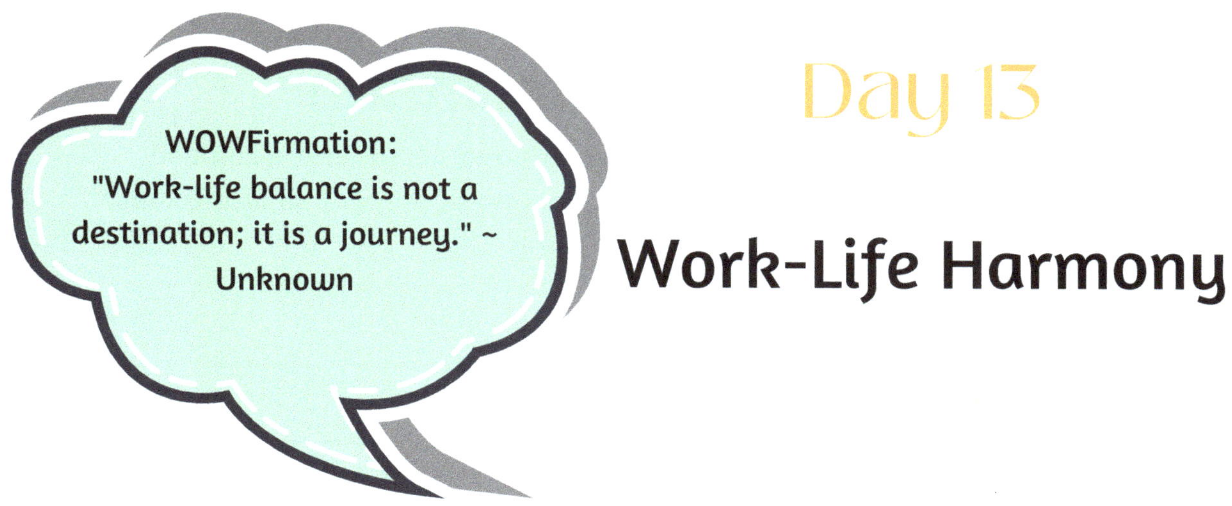

Introduction: Finding harmony between work and personal life can be challenging. Reflect on a recent situation where work and home life collided, and let's find ways to manage these situations better in the future.

Balance doesn't mean a perfect 50/50 split—it's about aligning your energy with your priorities and knowing when to shift gears. True harmony happens when your values lead the way and guilt takes a back seat. It requires boundaries, grace, and a willingness to reassess what matters most.

Think of a time when work and life blurred, and you felt pulled in multiple directions. What emotions came up? What would you do differently next time? These moments can reveal the tension between responsibility and rest, ambition and authenticity.

Today is an invitation to redefine what balance means to you—not what society says it should look like. Create a rhythm that feels sustainable, not exhausting. You deserve a life that supports your success and your sanity.

Harmony isn't about doing it all—it's about being fully present where you are. Let simple rituals guide your transitions, and trust yourself to realign as life ebbs and flows. Presence over perfection—that's where true balance lives.

Work-Life Harmony

Prompt: Describe a situation where work and personal life collided. How did you manage it, and what can you do to prevent similar issues?

Day 14

Self-Love Practice

Introduction: Self-love is a powerful tool for empowerment. Write yourself a love letter celebrating your strengths and achievements and think about how you can practice self-love more regularly.

Self-love isn't selfish—it's foundational. It's how you talk to yourself in quiet moments, how you treat your body, and how you set boundaries that protect your peace. It's knowing you are worthy even when you're still a work in progress.

Many of us wait for external validation, but the most meaningful recognition comes from within. When was the last time you paused to appreciate your resilience, your growth, or your light? You've come so far—and you deserve to celebrate that.

Take time today to write yourself a love letter. Let it be raw, real, and full of grace. Speak to yourself like someone you deeply admire. Let this be the start—or the deepening—of a beautiful relationship with you.

Self-love grows through repetition, not just reflection. Consider one small, daily ritual that reinforces this care—whether it's affirming yourself in the mirror, treating your body with kindness, or simply resting without guilt. These small moments compound into a deep sense of self-worth.

Self-Love Practice

Prompt: Write a love letter to yourself, acknowledging your strengths and achievements. How can you celebrate these aspects of yourself more often?

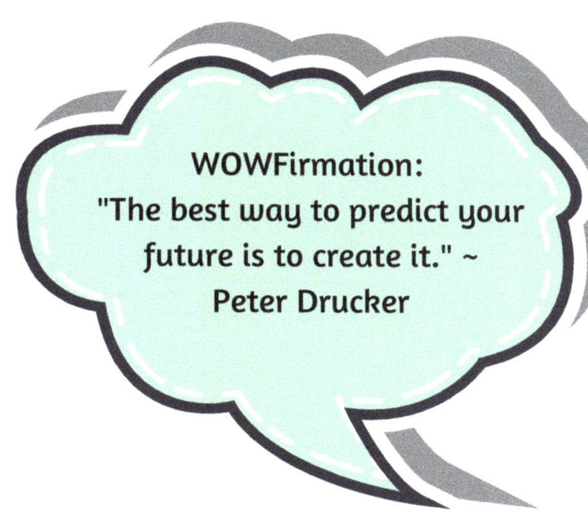

Financial Goals

Introduction: Setting financial goals can lead to greater security and less stress. Today, let's define a short-term financial goal and outline the steps to start working towards it.

Money isn't just math—it's mindset. Your financial goals are powerful tools for creating freedom, not just wealth. When you approach your finances with clarity and intention, you step into the role of creator rather than reactor.

What's one short-term goal that could bring you peace or progress? Maybe it's building a cushion in your savings, paying down a debt, or investing in something that nurtures your growth. It doesn't have to be big—it just has to matter to you.

Write it down and map out a few simple, doable steps. Remember, momentum builds confidence. With every decision you make from a place of intention, you're building a future that honors your values and your vision.

Your financial journey should feel aligned with your life, not like a punishment or restriction. Start by tracking where your money is currently going—awareness is the first step to transformation. Once you see the story your spending tells, you can begin rewriting it with purpose.

Celebrate progress over perfection—each intentional money choice is a step toward habits that honor your worth and support your well-being.

Financial Goals

Prompt: Set a short-term financial goal.
What steps will you take to achieve this goal?

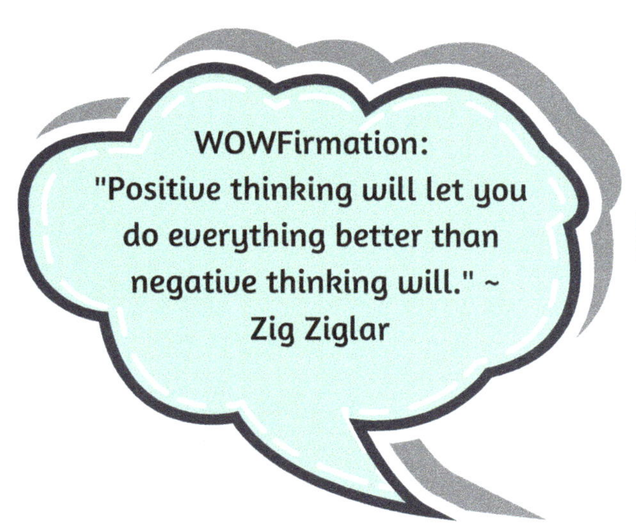

Day 16

Positivity Challenge

Introduction: A positive mindset can transform challenges into opportunities. Today, try a positivity challenge: find three positive aspects in a current challenge or stressor.

Positivity isn't pretending everything is perfect—it's choosing to look for the lessons and the light, even when things feel hard. It's a practice of perspective that trains your brain to focus on possibility, not just problems. Think of a current stressor or challenge. Now stretch yourself to find three things about that situation that are teaching you, growing you, or preparing you for something greater. This shift isn't always easy, but it is powerful.

Your mind is a garden—what you water will grow. Today, water the thoughts that lift you higher. Positivity won't make the hard stuff disappear, but it will give you the strength and clarity to face it with courage. Every time you choose a positive thought, you're not ignoring reality—you're reshaping it. Positivity gives you access to creativity, calm, and connection, even in chaos. This mindset doesn't just impact how you feel—it influences how you lead, relate, and rise.

Think of this challenge as emotional strength training. Just like building muscle, consistency matters more than intensity. When you seek the light daily—even in small doses—you build a deeper sense of confidence, gratitude, and inner peace that endures.

Positivity Challenge

Prompt: Identify a current challenge or stressor and list three positive aspects or opportunities within it.

Day 17

Personal Expression

Introduction: Expressing yourself authentically can be incredibly empowering. Today, write about a time when you were able to express yourself fully and how it made you feel.

Your voice holds power—not just in what you say, but in how you show up. Whether it's through words, style, creativity, or silence, expressing who you truly are is a radical act of self-ownership. Think back to a moment when you felt completely seen and heard. What allowed you to show up so fully? Was it a supportive space, a courageous decision, or a moment of clarity? When you stand in your truth, you give others permission to do the same.

Today is a chance to honor that version of you. The one who speaks up. The one who shares boldly. The one who refuses to shrink. Let your expression be a reflection of your brilliance—not your fear. Authentic expression often begins with self-awareness. It's knowing what you value, what you believe, and what lights you up. When you embrace your full identity without apology, you build deeper connections—because people can feel when you're being real.

Remember, personal expression doesn't have to be loud to be powerful. Sometimes it's the quiet courage to say "no," the boldness to wear what makes you feel alive, or the honesty in sharing your story. However you show up—let it be true to you.

Personal Expression

Prompt: Describe a time when you expressed yourself authentically.
How did it impact you and those around you?

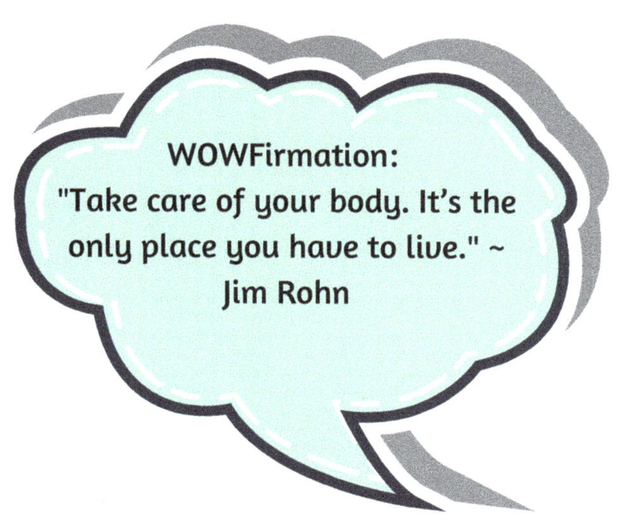

Self-Care Ritual

Introduction: Creating a self-care ritual can enhance your well-being. Choose one self-care activity you can do daily and commit to making it a part of your routine.

Self-care isn't just bubble baths and spa days—it's how you show yourself love and respect daily. It's a commitment to nourish your mind, body, and soul, even when life gets busy. A ritual doesn't have to be fancy—it just has to be yours. Maybe it's morning journaling, stretching before bed, drinking more water, digital detoxes, lighting a candle, or even talking kindly to yourself in the mirror. Small actions add up to big transformations over time.

Choose one simple ritual today. Practice it intentionally, not as another task but as an act of reverence for yourself. Let it remind you: you are worthy of care, every single day. Self-care is both preventive and restorative. It's not something you earn after burnout—it's what helps prevent it. Think of your chosen ritual as a daily deposit into your energy and emotional bank account. Over time, those small deposits create a powerful reserve of resilience.

And remember, self-care looks different for everyone. What restores you might not work for someone else—and that's okay. The most important part is choosing something that feels nourishing to you. The more personal it is, the more likely it is to become a lasting habit.

Self-Care Ritual

Prompt: Select one self-care activity to incorporate into your daily routine.
How will you ensure it becomes a regular part of your day?

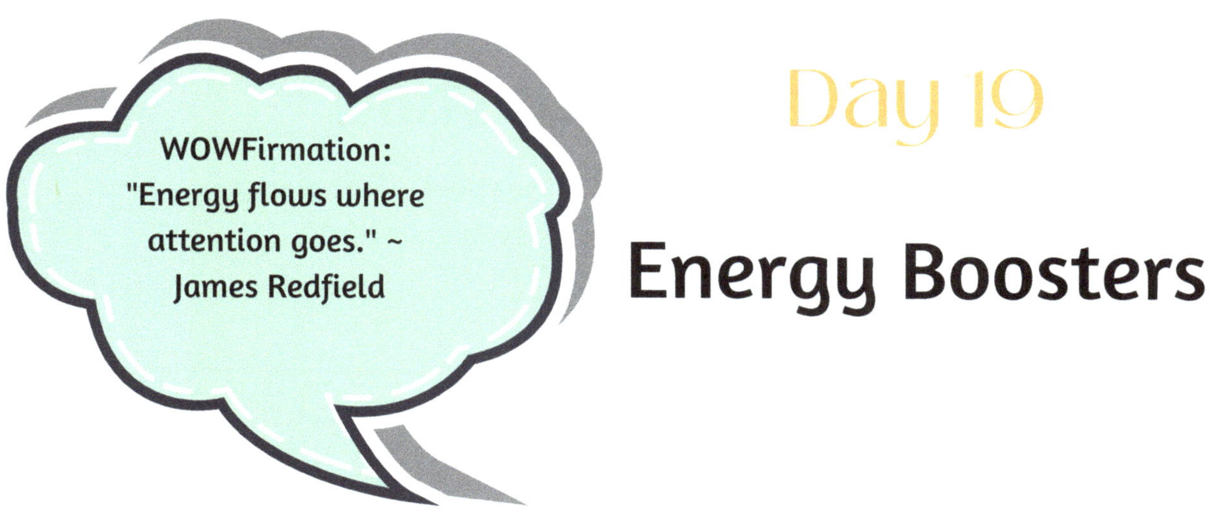

Day 19

Energy Boosters

Introduction: Focus on what energizes you. Reflect on activities or people that uplift you and consider how to prioritize these sources of positive energy.

Your energy is sacred—who and what you give it to matters. If you constantly feel drained, it's time to pause and reassess. What fills your cup? Who leaves you feeling inspired and alive?

Start by listing the people, places, and practices that give you a boost. Notice what patterns emerge. Is it nature? Music? Creative projects? Deep conversations? Alone time? Pay attention to what lights you up. Make a commitment to choose more of that. Protect your energy like the valuable asset it is. When you surround yourself with what uplifts you, you amplify your power—and that energy ripples into every area of your life.

Energy is not unlimited, but it is renewable. By consciously directing your attention to the sources that rejuvenate you, you create a sustainable cycle of motivation and vitality. This awareness helps you set boundaries and say no to energy drains that don't serve your highest good.

Remember, prioritizing your energy isn't selfish—it's essential. When you nurture your own vitality, you become a stronger, more present version of yourself, able to show up fully for your passions and the people who matter most.

Energy Boosters

Prompt: List activities or people that boost your energy.
How can you prioritize these in your life?

Financial Education

Introduction: Educating yourself about finances is empowering. Today, explore one financial topic that interests you and gather information to deepen your understanding.

Money confidence comes from financial clarity. You don't have to be an expert to take control of your finances—you just have to be curious and consistent. The more you know, the more choices you can make that reflect your values and goals.

Is there a topic you've been wanting to understand better—investing, budgeting, credit, taxes, or entrepreneurship? Choose one area that feels aligned with your current phase of life or future vision. Spend time today reading, listening to a podcast, or watching a video on that subject. Keep it simple. Every step you take toward understanding your finances is a step toward freedom, confidence, and ownership of your wealth story.

Financial education is not just about numbers—it's about empowerment. It gives you the language and tools to advocate for yourself, make decisions with intention, and build a future that reflects your dreams—not your fears.

Knowledge is a form of self-care and self-respect. When you learn how to manage and grow your money, you stop reacting and start leading. Let today be the spark that ignites your journey toward financial confidence and legacy building.

Financial Education

Prompt: Choose a financial topic you're curious about and research it.
What new insights have you gained?

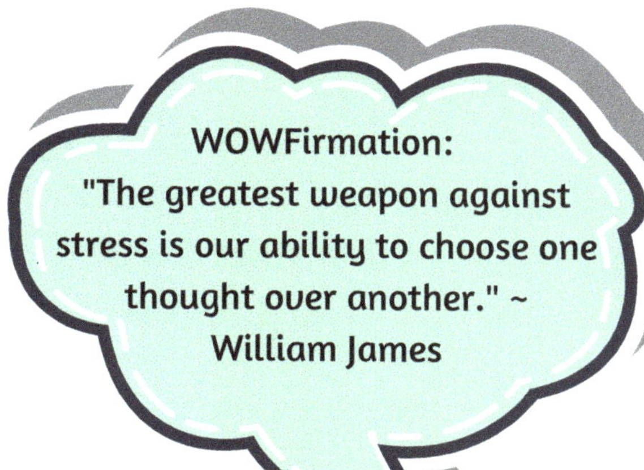

Day 21

Emotional Check-In

Introduction: Managing stress starts with awareness. Take a moment to check in with your emotions and identify any patterns that could be impacting your well-being.

Emotional check-ins are the pause points our minds and hearts crave. Often, we move through our routines on autopilot, brushing past the quiet whispers of our inner world. Today is about tuning in. Noticing what emotions have been quietly riding alongside you—whether it's joy, tension, irritation, or gratitude. Name it. Feel it. Welcome it without judgment.

When you give language to your emotions, you give yourself power. That awareness allows you to understand your reactions and tend to your deeper needs. Are you feeling drained by something unspoken? Is there a recurring thought that needs to be gently released? Emotional patterns often reveal where boundaries need to be strengthened or where healing is asking to begin. This exercise is not about fixing yourself—you are not broken. It's about understanding what you're holding so you can care for it with clarity and compassion. Your emotions are messengers, not burdens. Honor them today.

Think of emotional awareness as emotional hygiene—simple, daily check-ins that prevent stress buildup. Asking yourself, "How am I feeling right now?" can offer clarity and help you shift course with intention. Over time, these mindful moments build emotional resilience, helping you respond thoughtfully to your environment, protect your peace, and stay grounded through life's ups and downs.

Emotional Check-In

Prompt: Reflect on your current emotional state.
Are there any recurring patterns or triggers that affect your stress levels?

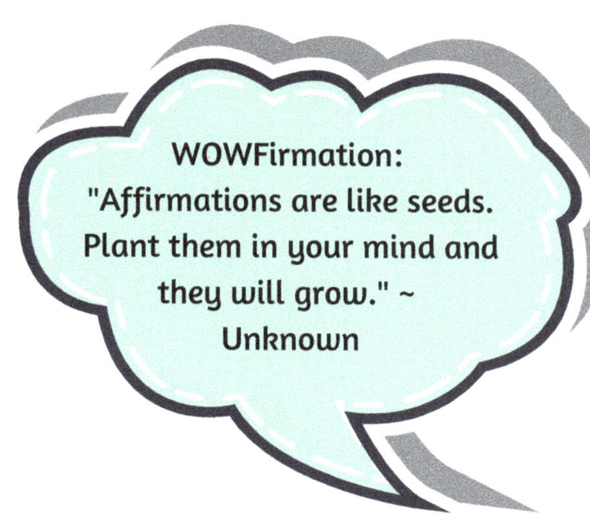

Day 22

Positive Affirmations

Introduction: Positive affirmations can shift your mindset. Create a list of affirmations that resonate with you and commit to reciting them daily.

Your words carry energy, and the ones you speak to yourself shape your reality. Affirmations aren't magic spells—they're reminders of truth, strength, and possibility. Each time you affirm something positive, you train your brain to look for evidence of that truth. That's how beliefs are formed: one repeated thought at a time.

Start with what you want to believe, even if it doesn't feel fully real yet. Maybe it's "I am worthy of rest," or "I trust myself to make wise decisions." Over time, these become internal anchors. Say them aloud. Write them. Post them where you'll see them.

Let today be a reset for your inner dialogue. Choose to speak to yourself like someone you love. The world is already full of noise—make your voice the one that uplifts.

Affirmations are most powerful when you truly feel them—don't just say the words, embody their energy. Stand taller with "I am powerful" or breathe deeply with "I am safe" to connect mind and body to the message. Consistency transforms these phrases from simple words into your inner soundtrack, reshaping your self-belief and, ultimately, your experience of life.

Positive Affirmations

Prompt: Write down three positive affirmations.
How can you incorporate them into your daily routine?

Day 23

Personal Values

Introduction: Understanding your core values helps align your actions with your true self. Reflect on what values are most important to you and how they influence your decisions.

Values are the compass points of your life's direction. When you feel out of alignment, chances are one of your core values is being ignored or compromised. That's why today is about digging deep and naming the principles that matter most to you.

Maybe you value honesty, freedom, creativity, or family. Whatever they are, these values should be reflected in your daily choices—from your relationships to your boundaries to how you spend your time. When you live in alignment with your values, peace follows. Today, define your top three values and explore how you can honor them more intentionally in your life.

Your values are more than ideals—they are the foundation of your integrity, motivation, and personal truth. When you clearly define what matters most, it becomes easier to say yes to what aligns and no to what doesn't. This clarity builds self-trust and eases decision-making, guiding you through life with confidence. Moments of fulfillment often signal values being honored, while frustration may reveal where they're being overlooked. Let today be your invitation to realign with what truly matters—so your choices reflect not just what you do, but who you are at your core.

Personal Values

Prompt: Identify your top three personal values.
How do these values shape your daily decisions and actions?

Self-Care Strategy

Introduction: A self-care strategy can prevent burnout. Assess your current self-care practices and identify any gaps that need to be addressed.

Self-care isn't just bubble baths and spa days—it's a commitment to your well-being. It's setting boundaries, taking mental health days, asking for help, and nourishing your body with rest and movement. It's checking in with what you need before you crash. Think of your self-care routine as a toolbox. What's in it right now? What's missing? What worked for you in the past that you might revisit? Today, design your ideal weekly self-care strategy. Include small, consistent actions and backup plans for when life gets busy. Your future self will thank you.

Your self-care strategy should reflect your lifestyle, your values, and your current capacity. It's not about adding more to your plate—it's about making room for what replenishes you. Even five-minute rituals, like a deep breath between meetings or a midday stretch, can make a significant impact when practiced regularly. The key is consistency over complexity.

Notice the warning signs your body and mind give when you're nearing burnout: fatigue, irritability, forgetfulness, or feeling disconnected. These aren't weaknesses—they're signals. Use them to adjust your rhythm, not punish yourself. When you prioritize yourself with care and compassion, you create the resilience needed to show up fully—for your work, your relationships, and most importantly, for you.

Self-Care Strategy

Prompt: Review your current self-care practices.
What adjustments can you make to improve your routine?

Financial Strategy

Introduction: A solid financial strategy is key to empowerment. Evaluate your current financial strategies and consider areas for improvement.

Money is more than math—it's mindset, emotion, and behavior. Creating a financial strategy is about clarity, not control. It helps reduce anxiety and increase your confidence in making empowered decisions. Start with a gentle inventory: What are your short-term financial goals? Where do your money habits support or sabotage those goals? Where can you educate yourself to feel more empowered? Whether it's building an emergency fund, tracking spending, or learning about investing, your next step doesn't have to be big. It just needs to be intentional.

Your financial strategy should support the life you want to live, not the life you think you should be living. That starts by aligning your money choices with your values and long-term vision. Budgeting doesn't have to mean restriction—it can be a roadmap to freedom. Clarity brings confidence, and small, consistent steps create lasting transformation.

Start paying attention to how money makes you feel—excited, anxious, avoidant, empowered. These emotional cues offer insight into your money story. By understanding your patterns and beliefs, you can begin to rewrite them. You don't need to have all the answers today, but you do need to stay curious, committed, and courageous with your finances.

Financial Strategy

Prompt: Assess your current financial strategies. What changes or improvements can you make to enhance your financial situation?

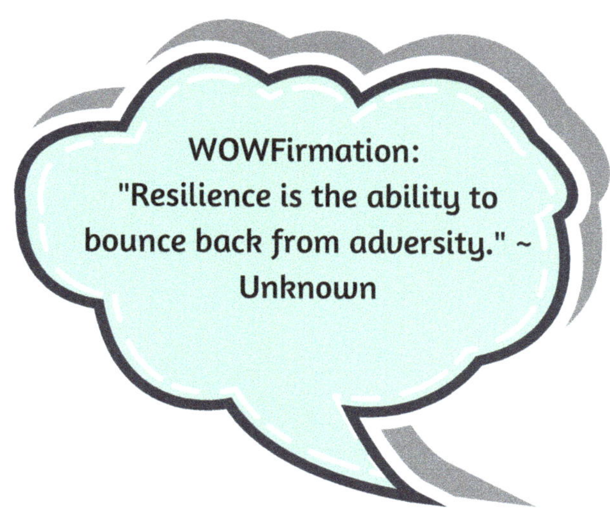

Day 26

Emotional Resilience

Introduction: Building emotional resilience helps you navigate challenges. Reflect on a recent setback and identify how you can develop greater resilience in similar situations.

Resilience doesn't mean never falling—it means rising again, wiser and stronger. Emotional resilience is a muscle. It grows when you face difficulty, name your emotions, and still choose to keep going.

Reflect on a moment that challenged you. How did you respond? What helped you recover? What would you do differently next time?
Resilience is also about support. Who can you lean on? What practices ground you? Build your bounce-back toolkit today.

Every challenge holds the potential to reveal your inner strength. The key is not to avoid discomfort, but to learn how to move through it with intention. Whether it's journaling, therapy, prayer, breathwork, or movement, resilience lives in your ability to return to center when life knocks you off balance.

Resilience also grows when you shift your inner dialogue. Instead of asking, "Why is this happening to me?" try asking, "What is this teaching me?" This perspective shift transforms obstacles into opportunities and equips you to meet future storms with greater courage, compassion, and clarity.

Emotional Resilience

Prompt: Describe a recent setback and how you responded.
What can you do to strengthen your emotional resilience?

Day 27

Personal Growth

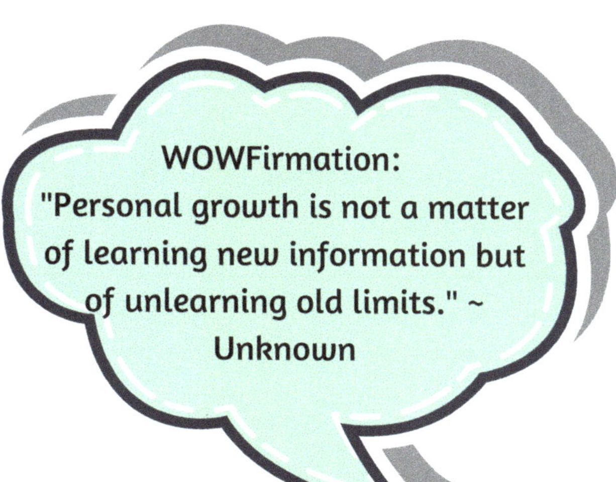

Introduction: Personal growth involves overcoming self-imposed limitations. Reflect on a belief or habit that may be holding you back and explore ways to overcome it.

Growth often means confronting what we've accepted as normal. That inner critic? That fear of visibility? That habit of shrinking when it's time to shine? All of it is learned—which means it can be unlearned. Think about an old story you've been telling yourself. Something like "I'm not good with money" or "I can't handle stress." Challenge it. Ask: Is this true? Or is this something I believed because I was trying to stay safe?

Growth starts when you choose to believe in something more expansive. Today is about planting a new narrative. Just like a plant needs pruning to thrive, personal growth often requires letting go of beliefs that once protected you but now limit your potential. These beliefs can be subtle—like perfectionism disguised as high standards, or self-doubt masked as humility. Growth happens when you begin replacing these outdated habits with empowering truths that align with who you're becoming.

This journey isn't about fixing yourself—it's about freeing yourself. When you approach growth with compassion and curiosity, you create space to evolve with grace. The more you release the beliefs that keep you small, the more you step into your full power. Start small. One belief. One shift. One brave choice at a time.

Personal Growth

Prompt: Identify a belief or habit that limits your personal growth.
How can you challenge or change it?

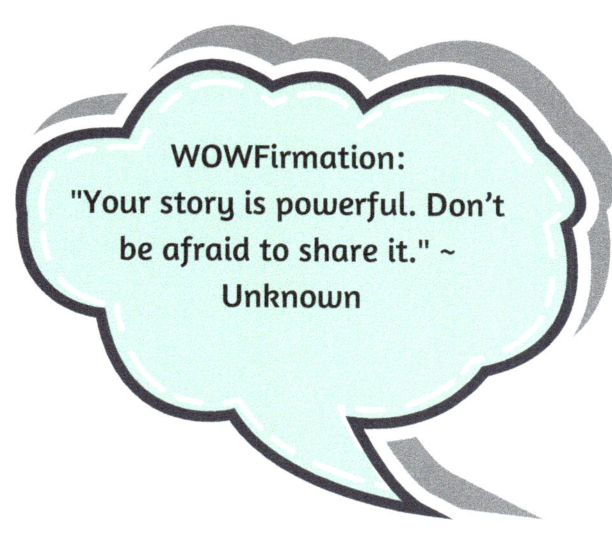

Day 28

Empowerment Through Expression

Introduction: Expressing your personal story can be empowering. Think about how sharing your experiences might inspire or impact others.

Your voice matters. Not just the polished version—the real, raw, beautiful truth of your journey. Every lesson, every detour, every breakthrough holds wisdom someone else might need to hear. Sharing your story doesn't have to mean a public platform. It could be in a journal, a trusted conversation, or even a creative outlet like art or poetry. The act of expression is healing.

Today, write a piece of your story you've never shared. What have you overcome? What have you learned? Let your voice lead. When you express your truth, you reclaim your power. Silence may have once been a survival strategy, but your growth invites a new way forward—one where your story is not hidden, but honored. Speaking your truth aloud, even just to yourself, affirms your worth and deepens your self-trust.

And as you share, you give others permission to do the same. Vulnerability becomes a bridge—connecting, healing, and empowering both the speaker and the listener. You never know who needs to hear your story to believe in their own. Let this be your reminder: what once made you feel alone may be the very thing that sets someone else free.

Empowerment Through Expression

Prompt: Write about a personal experience that has shaped who you are. How can sharing this story empower others or yourself?

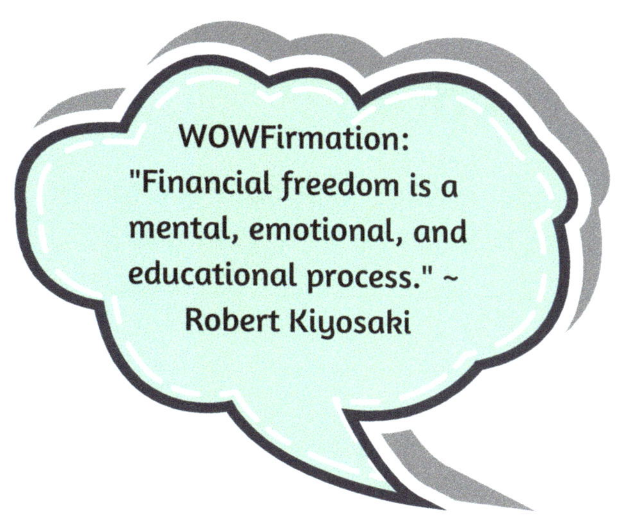

Financial Freedom

Introduction: Achieving financial freedom involves more than just numbers. Reflect on your journey towards financial freedom and what steps you need to take to continue progressing.

Financial freedom is about choice—the freedom to spend your time and energy in ways that align with your purpose. It starts with mindset. Do you believe it's possible for you? Freedom also means understanding your numbers, healing your money story, and creating systems that support long-term growth. What does freedom look like for you—time flexibility? Debt-free living? Legacy building?

Define your version of financial freedom and take one aligned action today.
Define your version of financial freedom and take one aligned action today.

True financial freedom begins with clarity: knowing what you value, what you're working toward, and what you're willing to shift in order to get there. Whether you're paying off debt, saving for a dream, or learning how to invest, each step you take is a declaration that you believe in your ability to thrive.

Let this be your reminder: freedom isn't a final destination—it's a daily practice. Every time you choose intention over impulse, awareness over avoidance, and courage over fear, you move closer to the life you envision. Financial freedom is built one decision, one belief, one bold move at a time.

Financial Freedom

Prompt: Reflect on your path to financial freedom. What steps have you taken, and what additional actions can you take to move closer to your goal?

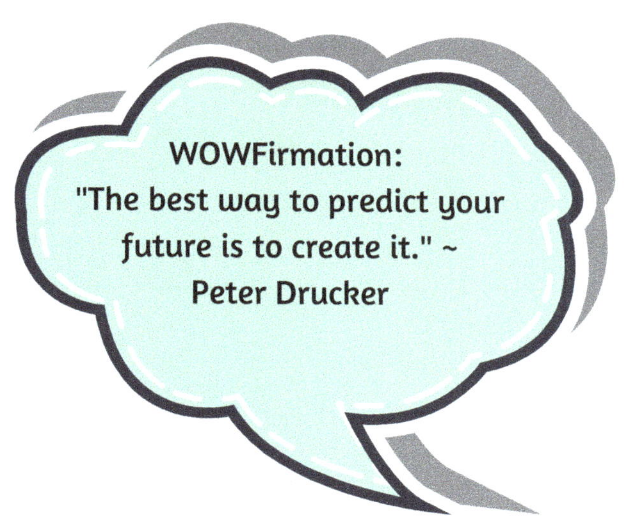

Reflection and Celebration

Introduction: Congratulations on completing your 30-day journey! Take time to reflect on your progress, celebrate your achievements, and set intentions for the future.

You did it. You committed to yourself, and that matters. This journey has been about more than writing prompts—it's been a declaration of your worth, your growth, and your power to create change. Take a moment to look back. What surprised you? What shifted? What do you want to carry forward?

Celebrate your wins, big or small. Honor your effort. You are no longer who you were on Day 1—you're even more aligned with your brilliance. Now, let that brilliance guide your next chapter.

Reflection gives power to the progress you've made. As you look back over the past 30 days, notice the themes that emerged, the insights that landed, and the resilience that carried you through. Growth isn't always loud—it's often in the subtle mindset shifts, the reclaimed boundaries, and the renewed self-trust.

Let this final day serve as both a pause and a launch. You've planted seeds of clarity, courage, and confidence. Now, commit to nurturing them. Whether your next step is rest, reinvention, or reaching higher, you have the tools—and the truth—to move forward with intention.

Reflection and Celebration

Prompt: Reflect on your journey over the past 30 days.
What are you most proud of, and what goals do you want to set for the future?

AFFIRMATIONS

Positivity

1. "I embrace each day with a positive attitude and an open heart."
2. "I choose to see the good in every situation and person."
3. "I radiate positivity and attract uplifting energy into my life."
4. "I am grateful for the abundance of positive experiences in my life."
5. "I focus on solutions rather than dwelling on problems."
6. "I turn challenges into opportunities for growth and learning."
7. "I maintain a positive outlook, even in the face of adversity."
8. "I find joy and beauty in the little things every day."
9. "I surround myself with positive influences and supportive people."
10. "I believe in my ability to create a positive and fulfilling life."

Self-Love

1. "I am worthy of love and respect just as I am."
2. "I embrace my imperfections and see them as part of my unique beauty."
3. "I nurture my mind, body, and spirit with kindness and compassion."
4. "I celebrate my achievements and acknowledge my worth."
5. "I forgive myself for past mistakes and focus on my growth."
6. "I honor my feelings and give myself permission to express them."
7. "I am my own biggest supporter and cheerleader."
8. "I practice self-love by setting healthy boundaries and prioritizing my needs."
9. "I am deserving of all the love and happiness life has to offer."
10. "I continuously grow and evolve into the best version of myself."

Personal Expression

1. "I confidently express my thoughts and ideas with clarity and courage."
2. "I value my unique voice and contribute it to the world."
3. "I am open to sharing my creativity and passions with others."
4. "I communicate authentically and with purpose in all areas of my life."
5. "I embrace my individuality and let it shine in everything I do."
6. "I am proud of my personal expression and the impact it has on others."
7. "I listen to my inner voice and honor its guidance."
8. "I use my personal expression to inspire and uplift those around me."
9. "I celebrate the diversity of voices and perspectives in my life."
10. "I trust in my ability to express myself creatively and meaningfully."

AFFIRMATIONS Cont'd:

Self-Care

1. "I prioritize my well-being and make time for self-care every day."
2. "I listen to my body and respond with nurturing actions."
3. "I create a balanced life by integrating self-care into my routine."
4. "I am worthy of relaxation and rest, and I embrace them without guilt."
5. "I practice self-care with love and intention, knowing it enhances my overall health."
6. "I take time to engage in activities that bring me joy and fulfillment."
7. "I set aside time for myself and honor it as a vital part of my routine."
8. "I nourish my body with healthy food, exercise, and adequate rest."
9. "I create a peaceful and restorative environment in my daily life."
10. "I commit to ongoing self-care as an essential aspect of my personal growth."

Financial Empowerment

1. "I take control of my financial future with confidence and clarity."
2. "I make informed and thoughtful decisions about my finances."
3. "I am empowered to create and achieve my financial goals."
4. "I am grateful for the abundance in my life and manage it wisely."
5. "I invest in myself and my future with financial prudence."
6. "I maintain a positive attitude towards money and abundance."
7. "I track my spending and savings to ensure financial stability."
8. "I am capable of creating and sustaining financial success."
9. "I approach financial challenges with a proactive and solution-oriented mindset."
10. "I celebrate my financial achievements and continue to strive for growth and prosperity."

About the Author

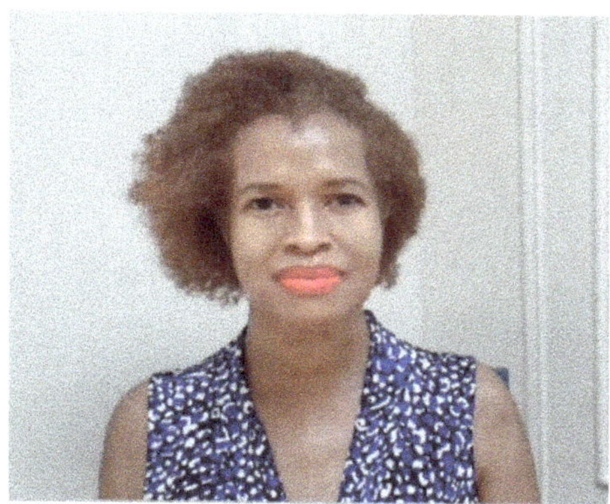

Sheryll Mizell is a global speaker, international best-selling author, and host of WakeUP to Your W.O.W.!®. As the visionary leader of Fit For Biz® Consulting, Inc., she's redefining holistic financial empowerment for high-achieving individuals and entrepreneurs.

With 15 years in financial services and HR, she helps leaders blend profits with purpose and wellness with leadership. A resilience and burnout prevention expert, she equips others to rise above overwhelm, lead with authenticity, and reclaim their energy. She is redefining what it means to thrive in business and beyond. Thriving, she believes, isn't about doing more—it's about doing what matters, in ways that are aligned, sustainable, and soul-honoring.

In June 2025, Sheryll will be awarded an Honorary Doctorate in Humanitarianism, honoring her dedication to elevating voices, transforming communities, and leading with heart-centered purpose. Through her work, she empowers lasting change—sparking personal breakthroughs and ripple effects of healing and leadership.

In a world that often equates strength with hardness, she chooses a different path—one rooted in presence, joy, and radical softness. Whether dancing to her own rhythm, skipping down city streets, or pausing to savor life's quiet moments, she lives as a reminder: softness is not weakness—it is grounded, intentional strength. It's not just how she lives; it's what she teaches.

Thank you for being part of the WakeUP to Your W.O.W.!® journey.
 For more resources, journal updates, and connection opportunities, visit:
https://linktr.ee/SheryllMizell

Questions or collaborations? Reach out: mizellcan@gmail.com

Additional Notes